Disney
PRINCESS

# CELEBRATE
## with Moana

## Plan a Wayfinding Party

Niki Ahrens

Lerner Publications ◆ Minneapolis

## For Eliza

Lerner Publications Company
An imprint of Lerner Publishing Group, Inc.
241 First Avenue North
Minneapolis, MN 55401 USA

For reading levels and more information, look up this title at www.lernerbooks.com.

Main body text set in Billy Infant.
Typeface provided by Sparky Type.

### Library of Congress Cataloging-in-Publication Data

Names: Ahrens, Niki, 1979- author.
Title: Celebrate with Moana: plan a wayfinding party / Niki Ahrens.
Description: Minneapolis, MN: Lerner Publications Company, [2020] | Series: Disney princess celebrations | Includes bibliographical references and index. | Audience: Age 6-10. | Audience: Grades K to 3.
Identifiers: LCCN 2019011421 (print) | LCCN 2019013583 (ebook) | ISBN 9781541582781 (eb pdf) | ISBN 9781541572737 (lb : alk. paper)
Subjects: LCSH: Party decorations—Juvenile literature. | Children's parties—Juvenile literature. | Moana (Motion picture)—Juvenile literature. | Polynesia—Social life and customs—Juvenile literature.
Classification: LCC TT900.P3 (ebook) | LCC TT900.P3 A45 2020 (print) | DDC 745.594/1—dc23

LC record available at https://lccn.loc.gov/2019011421

Manufactured in the United States of America
1-46540-47585-7/22/2019

# Table of Contents

# A Wayfinding Party

To help her people, Moana journeys across the ocean.
Celebrate exploration and discovery by leading a
*Moana*-inspired party! Here's what you'll need to do:

- ◎ Ask a parent or guardian for permission to throw a party, and pick a time and place. Send your invitations!

- ◎ Plan and make decorations, party favors, and treats. Clean up before your celebration.

- ◎ Lead your party activities fearlessly!

- ◎ After the journey, clean your party space, and send thank-you notes to your guests.

# Party Host Tips!

- 🌀 Be considerate by asking your guests about food allergies.

- 🌀 Respect your space by covering the table with newspaper before making party materials.

- 🌀 Be responsible with food. Wash your hands before prepping food, and ask an adult for help when you need it.

- 🌀 Be sure to include all your guests as you bravely lead the fun.

- 🌀 Help nature by recycling any materials that you can after the celebration.

# Boat Voyage Invitations

Moana sets sail on an adventurous ocean journey. Make boat invitations that welcome your guests to your celebration.

## Materials

- 11 wooden craft sticks for each invitation

- craft glue

- scissors

- white paper for each invitation

- pen

- red crayon

1. Set 9 craft sticks side by side, touching on the long sides.

2. Glue a craft stick straight across the other 9 sticks about 0.5 inches (1.25 cm) from the top. Glue another stick about 0.5 inches from the bottom.

3. Allow the glue to dry completely.

4. Cut out a 4-inch (10 cm) square of white paper. Write your invitation on the paper square. Include the date, time, and place!

5. Fold your square in half, matching opposite points to make a triangle. Decorate the outside of your triangle sail with the crayon.

6. Tuck a corner of your sail between 2 parallel craft sticks.

7. Make an invitation for each guest!

### Party Tip! Did You Know?

Most kinds of wood are buoyant. This means they float on water. Your guests can float their boat invitations!

# Shiny Tamatoa Decoration

Tamatoa is so shiny! Make your party sparkle with Tamatoa and his twinkling treasures.

## Materials

- medium-size paintbrush

- purple tempera paint

- white construction paper

- muffin liner

- glue stick

- foil pieces

- 2 googly eyes

- pen

1. Use the paintbrush to paint the palm of your hand with purple paint.

2. Spread apart your fingers, and carefully stamp your hand on the paper to make a handprint. Wash your hand.

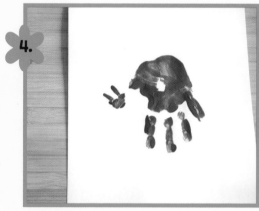

3. Turn the paper so the fingers of the handprint are pointing down and the thumb is pointing to the side. The fingers will be Tamatoa's legs, and the thumb will be his head.

4. Paint 2 short lines going up from the top of your stamped thumb.

5. While the paint dries, flatten a muffin liner, and glue shiny pieces of foil to one side of it to create a shell.

6. Glue the shiny shell to the palm of the dry handprint.

7. Glue a googly eye to the end of each of the lines above your thumbprint.

8. Use the pen to draw Tamatoa's mouth on your thumbprint.

9. Hang your Tamatoa decoration in your party space.

# Island Smoothies

The people of Motunui count on their island for food and shelter. Serve tasty island smoothies using tropical treats.

## Materials

• blender

• 1 juice glass for each guest

## Ingredients

*This recipe makes 8 4-ounce (237 mL) servings.*

• ⅔ cup coconut milk

• 1 banana

• 2 cups frozen mango or pineapple pieces

• 3 cups pineapple juice

1. Wash your hands before you work with food in the kitchen, and ask an adult for help with the blender. Remember, the blades are sharp!

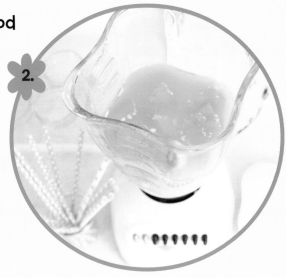

2. Carefully add the coconut milk, banana, frozen fruit, and pineapple juice to the blender.

3. Blend until the treat looks smooth and you don't see any chunks of fruit.

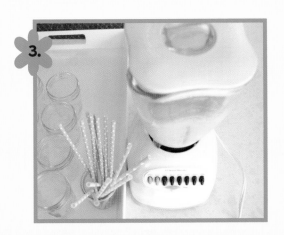

4. Carefully pour the smoothies into juice glasses.

5. Serve your guests refreshing smoothies!

# Shape-Shifting Fun

Maui transforms into different shapes. Practice
your shape-shifting skills with modeling dough,
and play a guessing game at your party.

## Materials

- large mixing bowl

- mixing spoon

- 2 cups flour

- ½ cup salt

- 2 tablespoons cream of tartar

- 1 cup warm water

- food coloring

- plastic bag

- cookie cutters or plastic knives
  (optional)

1. Before the celebration, prepare the dough. In the large bowl, mix the flour, salt, cream of tartar, and warm water until a dough forms.

2. Carefully mix in food coloring. Add 5 to 10 drops at a time until you have a color you like. Seal in a plastic bag until your guests arrive.

3. During the party, give each guest some dough. Playing at a table works best.

4. Make shapes and then transform them into something new. You can use cookie cutters or plastic knives to help shape the dough.

5. Take turns guessing everyone's creations!

## Party Tip! Be Respectful
Help every guest feel included by using only friendly words. Send a bag of modeling dough home with your friends!

# Wayfinding Adventure

Moana discovers her people's lost art of wayfinding. Lead a fun mapmaking adventure game that your guests will love.

## Materials

- paper clips

- sheets of paper about 8.5 x 11 inches (22 x 28 cm)

- pieces of cardboard about 8.5 x 11 inches

- pencil for each guest

1. Before the party, use a paper clip to attach one sheet of paper to the top of a cardboard panel for each guest.

2. Have an adult help you identify safe mapmaking boundaries for the activity.

3. At the party, ask your guests to map out a unique path from one point to another within your game space. Have them do this by drawing a starting point object and then adding 5 important hints along their chosen path.

## Party Tip! Did you know?

Early Pacific Islanders did not have compasses or Global Positioning Systems (GPS). They used wayfinding when they sailed. They followed the stars, ocean currents, wind patterns, and more to find their way!

4. When everyone finishes mapmaking, invite guests to pair up. Partners will exchange maps and try to navigate each other's mapped path.

5. Switch partners and try again.

# Heart of Te Fiti Party Favors

Moana restores the Heart of Te Fiti to save her island. Send guests on a safe journey home with this heartwarming keepsake.

## Materials

- medium paintbrush

- 2- to 3-inch (5 to 7.6 cm) wooden disk or smooth stone for each guest

- green paint

- silver permanent marker

1. Use the paintbrush to paint the face-up side of the disk or stone with green paint. Allow the paint to dry.

2. Flip the disk or stone over, and paint the other side. Allow this side to dry completely too.

3. Use the silver marker to draw a Heart of Te Fiti swirl symbol on one side of the stone or disk.

**4.** Make a special party favor
for each of your guests!

## Party Tip! Be Earth-Friendly
Instead of using wooden disks or
stones, you could find recycled bottle
caps, cardboard circles, or jar lids to
make into party favors.

# Ocean Thank-You Paintings

Moana is thankful for the Ocean's friendship and help. Make waves when you thank your guests with an Ocean painting.

## Materials

- 1 sheet of white card stock per guest

- white crayon

- small or medium paintbrush

- watercolor paints

- pen or marker

1. Fold a sheet of card stock in half, matching its shorter sides.

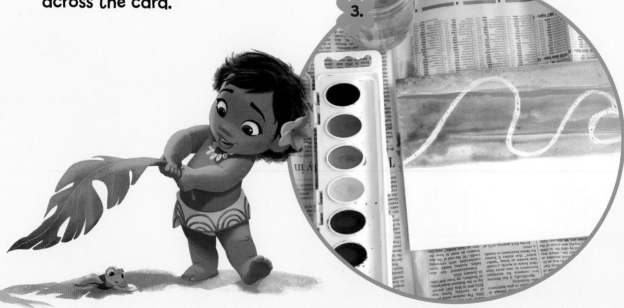

2. Use the white crayon to draw some waves on the cover of your folded card. Draw on top of your lines again to make thick, raised wave lines.

3. Use the paintbrush and watercolor paints to paint ocean colors across the front of the card. Change the color to a lighter or darker shade of ocean water, such as blue, purple, or green, to make different stripes across the card.

4. Allow your card to dry completely.

5. Open your card and write a thank-you message inside.

6. Send an Ocean note to each of your guests.

# Find Your Way

As Moana sets out to save her people, she learns about their past and shapes their future. She is determined to improve island life for everyone.

How could your party celebrate brave journeys? Find inspiration in Moana's courage, and plan a party that feels meant for you. Where will your imagination lead you? Have fun finding your way!

# Glossary

**buoyant:** capable of floating

**current:** the flow of water

**determined:** set to work toward a goal even when it's difficult

**Global Positioning System (GPS):** a navigation system that uses signals from satellites to tell you where you are and to give you directions to other places

**guest:** someone who attends a person's event or party

**host:** person who holds an event or party

**keepsake:** a meaningful item that is given or kept

**transform:** to change completely

**wayfinding:** the techniques developed by early Pacific Islanders to travel across the ocean

# To Learn More

## BOOKS

Ahrens, Niki. Moana *Idea Lab.* Minneapolis: Lerner Publications, 2020. Enjoy hands-on STEAM projects inspired by *Moana*.

Dichter, Paul. *The Pacific Islands: A* Moana *Discovery Book.* Minneapolis: Lerner Publications, 2019. Explore the Pacific Islands including the history of the islands, the many cultures of the people who live there, and their ways of life.

## WEBSITES

Everything You Need to Know before Seeing *Moana*
https://ohmy.disney.com/movies/2016/11/22/everything-you
-need-to-know-before-seeing-moana/
Learn about the lively characters, music, and setting of *Moana*.

Quiz: Get 100% on This Quiz to Prove You're the Ultimate *Moana* Fan
https://ohmy.disney.com/quiz/2017/07/28/quiz-get-100-on
-this-quiz-to-prove-youre-the-ultimate-moana-fan/
Take this challenging *Moana* quiz to show how much you know about the movie.

# Index

## PHOTO CREDITS

Additional photo credits: art_of_sun/Shutterstock.com, p. 2; Julia Sudnitskaya/ Shutterstock.com, p. 3; udra11/Shutterstock.com, p. 5T; wavebreakmedia/Shutterstock.com, p. 5B; nioloxs/Shutterstock.com, p. 7T; Gitchasron Thantupsron/EyeEm/Getty Images, p. 7B. Cover and design elements: Susii/Shutterstock.com (balloons); YamabikaY/Shutterstock.com (glitter); surachet khamsuk/Shutterstock.com (glitter).